For Emma Elizabeth Harding

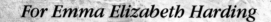

Henry Holt and Company, Inc.
Publishers since 1866
115 West 18th Street
New York, New York 10011

Henry Holt is a registered
trademark of Henry Holt and Company, Inc.

Published in Canada by Fitzhenry & Whiteside Ltd.,
195 Allstate Parkway, Markham, Ontario L3R 4T8.
Originally published in the United Kingdom in 1993
by ABC (All Books for Children), a division of
the All Children's Company Ltd., London.

Library of Congress Card Catalog Number: 93-78609
ISBN: 0-8050-3059-X

First American Edition—1994
Printed in Hong Kong

1 3 5 7 9 10 8 6 4 2

Cock-a-doodle-doo!

Emma Harding

Henry Holt and Company • *New York*

Cock-a-doodle-doo!

My dame has
lost her shoe,

My master's lost
his fiddling stick,

And knows not
what to do.

Cock-a-doodle-doo!

What is my dame to do?

Till master finds his fiddling stick
She'll dance without her shoe.

Cock-a-doodle-doo!

My dame has found her shoe,

And master's found
his fiddling stick,

Sing doodle-doodle-doo.

Cock-a-doodle-doo!

My dame will
dance with you,
While master fiddles
his fiddling stick

For dame and doodle-doo.